Small Talk

1000 bits of stuff & nonsense

Kasey RT Graham

First Printing, 2016

ISBN-13: 978-1533452627
ISBN-10: 1533452628

This is a work of humor and satire. Names, characters, businesses, places, events, products, and incidents are used in a fictitious or satirical manner.

Direct all questions and comments to:
                smalltalkchatter@gmail.com

<u>**CONTENTS**</u>

Introduction

Dear readers (both of you),

Please take this book as you would a margarita: with a grain of salt. Or 6 - 7 times before passing out on the bathroom floor. It is silly, nonsensical, ridiculous, and if you squint while skimming, profoundly deep.

The collection is dedicated to three special men:

Ian Liberto is my heart and soul. He laughs too hard at my duds and not at all at my best material. He is the butt of 30% of this book, and boy, what a butt!

In 2011, Ian's father, Tony Liberto passed away from complications from Non-Hodgkin's Lymphoma. I had been searching for a way to honor the memory of an incredible father, husband, and human and eventually landed on this collection.

A month after I started compiling material, I met a young man named Ryan Marston in Toronto. He was battling Hodgkin's Lymphoma. Plainly stated, he was the coolest person I've ever met. His humor was dark; his heart was luminous. He left too soon, but he changed me irrevocably.

50% of all proceeds from *Small Talk* go to cancer charities. If you like the book, tell your friends. If you hate it, tell your enemies.

And be good to each other.

Kasey RT Graham

Chapter 1
Senseless Wordplay

1.

I give people with a limp the benefit of the gout.

2.

One might call the Amish a clothes-knit community.

3.

I collect footstools in the hopes of one day having an Ottoman Empire.

4.

I'm a Venture Capitalist.
I always capitalize the word *Venture*.

5.

Wouldn't you hate to be the one unfit fiddle who proves the rule?

6.

I searched everywhere for my gloves,
but I came up empty-handed.

7.

I don't think I'm cut out for paper doll work.

8.

I could never hire a prostitute.
I'm not buysexual.

9.

I tried throwing shade once.
My sunglasses broke.

10.

My breadsticks are so hot,
they could be roll models.

11.

I'd like to be a census-taking Ninja,
so my job would literally be *kicking ass
and taking names*.

12.

I've cornered the market on right angles.

13.

If this is a colonoscopy,
I want a *semi*-colonoscopy.

14.

A graffiti removal service would clean up
in Manhattan.

15.

I hate to jump to conclusions,
but sometimes it's the most efficient
way to get to them.

16.

"There are going to be sweeping changes
around here!"
— An Ambitious Maid

17.

Venn diagrams are quite popular in
certain circles.

18.

I'm kind of anal about my bowel movements.

19.

Yoga instructors make the best friends.
They'll bend over backwards for you.

20.

Designing cul-de-sacs is a dead-end job.

21.

I broke down and visited the waterfront.
I've never been good with pier pressure.

22.

My suburban apartment is giving me a complex.

23.

I swallowed a firefly on my run.
I wanted to eat light, but this is ridiculous.

24.

I'm not a consistent beach-lover.
It comes in waves.

25.
Vegetarians:
Speak now, or forever hold your peas.

26.
I tried to learn about paving techniques,
but there aren't a lot of concrete absolutes.

27.
You know what gets a bad wrap?
Presents from straight guys.

28.
At least when an underwear salesman stops by,
you know he'll be brief.

29.
I'm obsessed with office supplies.
You could call me a file-ophile.

30.
I've done a complete 180 on U-turns.

31.
My paranoia about over-sleeping is alarm-ing.

32.

I wanted to open a small business selling cozy homes, but it's really more of a cottage industry.

33.

I can't spell my way out of a paypur bagg.

34.

Thank God for pencil sharpeners.
Never a dull moment!

35.

Joan of Arc sued the firemen for
de-flammation of character.

36.

That witch isn't wicked,
she just has Crone's Disease.

37.

I'm on the fence about property lines.

38.

Attorneys have the best will power.

39.

Petty cash must feel so down on itself.

40.

I'm thinking about studying abroad,
but I can't decide *which* broad.

41.

I can't take anything a plastic surgeon says at
face value.

42.

My microwave never shies away from the
hot button issues.

43.

Someday I'll open a hearing aide store called
Hear Here!

44.

I was going to post a joke about the Invisible Man,
but my motive was transparent.

45.

Are peonies potted trained?
Asking for a frond.

46.

Yes! This hammer is nailing it!

47.

Starting a thought with a proper noun is a
Capital Idea!

48.

Hula-hoops have really come full circle.

49.

Beware of gifts wearing fake glasses:
They could be blessings, in disguise.

50.

I searched the city for an oven mitt,
but I was looking for glove in all the
wrong places.

Chapter 2
Fun & Games

51.
I'm returning the NRA board game
I accidentally bought:
Shoots, Ladders, and Ask Questions Later.

52.
I ate a *Monopoly*® piece.
It was a little gamey.

53.
How has Vanna White not been replaced
by PowerPoint?

54.
I speak with no medical authority,
but I wager dyslexic people are far superior when
it comes to Word Jumbles.

55.
When did *Celebrity Jeopardy* turn into
Where Are They Now Jeopardy?

56.

If you pregame alone, is it solitaire
or alcoholism?

57.

I highly doubt that actual
naval captains ever cry,
"You sunk my battleship!"

58.

Let's play *Water, Coffee, or Urine*,
the sidewalk guessing game that's sweeping
San Francisco!

59.

Octomom giving birth must've looked like a
spirited game of *Whack-a-Mole®*.

60.

I love Crossword Puzzles,
but I hate...shit, what are they called...Oh, right!
Word Searches.

61.

It sucks playing *Cranium*™ with Michelangelo.
His cloodles take over a year to complete.

62.

Lucy and Ethel:
The ultimate Candy Crushers.

63.

Jambo means *Hello.*
Jenga® means *That tower will fall on your turn.*

64.

I was going to play a card game naked,
but it was *Taboo*®.

65.

"You complete me."
– 5/6 of the *Trivial Pursuit* pie
to the final slice

66.

"I can guess that song in one note."
– Gregorian Monk
on *Name That Tune*

67.

Clue is a 1949 children's game centered on
murdering colorful characters in various rooms.
It was a simpler time.

68.

We could play with an 80's toy,
or we could just Skip-It®.

69.

I set up 4 hands of *Uno*™ on the coffee table,
so the delivery guy doesn't think all the
food is for me.

70.

Be warned:
If you're not telling a story fast enough,
I'll start mad-libbing it *for* you.

71.

Violence is never the answer,
so stop guessing it on *The Family Feud!*

72.

I just learned you can play Gin Rummy sober,
and it's a game-changer.

73.

If we're being honest, *Dungeons & Dragons*
should be called *Mom's Basement & Ferrets.*

74.

I've never seen *Game of Thrones*,
but I *have* played Pictionary® on the toilet
if that counts.

75.

Some parents give their kids the
*Birds and the Be*es talk.
Mine gave me *Twister*® and a little privacy.

76.

"Bob Barker needs to mind his own
damn business."

– The Pet Population

77.

Operation™ is great practice for medical school,
if you don't mind doctors who flip the f*** out
when they buzz your insides trying to
remove your funny bone.

78.

I played telephone on my wedding night.
By the time it got back to me, it was still,
"Not tonight, I have a headache."

79.

I'm so naive, every night for over a year,
I watched *The $100,000 Pyramid Scheme*.

80.

Monopoly® ruins friendships,
but only because the game lasts so long,
players realize they never had anything in
common to begin with.

81.

Most likely, Alex Trebek would do better on
Wheel of Fortune than Pat Sajak would do
on *Jeopardy*.

82.

"I'll take the physical challenge," is the 2nd worst
Nickelodian® catchphrase I've blurted on a date.

83.

I'm still trying to get the slime out of the curtains
from the 1st worst.

84.

The game *Guess Who* teaches children –
don't pick the guy with glasses.

Chapter 3
Movies & Hollywood

85.

I never saw *Can't Hardly Wait*,
which proves that I could.

86.

It was quite respectful of the Beast not to use his
magic mirror to watch Belle shower.

87.

Being an adult means siding a little more with
Sally Field in *Mrs. Doubtfire.*

88.

I can never see *Showgirls* again.
Watching an actress with two different
emotions is exhausting.

89.

I get why Ariel can't walk. (She's a mermaid.)
But why does she have such a poor grasp on
English, when it seems to be her
native language.

90.

I'm rising,
but I'll leave the shining to Jack Nicholson.

91.

I saw *Heathers*, and Winona Ryder
stole the movie.
Literally.

92.

C-3PO and R2-D2 are the Bert and Ernie of
outer space.

93.

I might write a movie about a cutthroat shoe sale:
Last of the Moccasins.

94.

I don't even want to know what the balloon
payment mortgage was on that house from *UP*.

95.

The Breakfast Club is too much club and
too little breakfast for my taste.

96.

Learning a new skill in a movie never takes
longer than a two-song montage.
I see you, *Dirty Dancing*.

97.

When I take a bath, I splash
around like Daryl Hannah.
Not Daryl Hannah from *Splash*.
Just regular ol' Daryl Hannah.

98.

I don't blame Bruce Willis,
but the opening credits sequence in
Look Who's Talking absolutely turned me gay.

99.

I want to live in romantic comedies:
A world where morning breath doesn't exist.

100.

Nothing gives me anxiety quite like wondering
which Disney™ film will go into the vault next.

101.

1997's *Spice World* is a tale as old as thyme.

102.

I want to write a movie in which
Jason Bourne time travels:
Bourne Yesterday.

103.

My postman is so aggressive,
he always rings thrice.

104.

I didn't grow up with a lot of brand name items.
All Frogs Go to Heaven was my favorite VHS tape.

105.

If one were taught how to properly train
one's dragon the first time,
the sequels wouldn't be necessary.

106.

Viola Davis is getting so much buzz,
Meryl Streep will play her one day.

107.

I wish I were Tom Cruise and Katie Holmes's child.
Sorry not Suri.

108.

If I were Marie, I'd tell that baker,
"You'll get these damn baguettes when I'm
good and ready!"

109.

After watching *9 to 5*,
I always suffer from post-Parton depression.

110.

I thought the guy running this cafe was gay,
until he told a customer his favorite
movie was *Son of the Mask*.

111.

If all movie titles were as on the nose
as *Home Alone*,
the world would be a better place.
Looking at you, *Monster's Ball*.

112.

I just had a near miss with a roller-blader.
I wasn't clear on sidewalk etiquette,
as I haven't seen a roller-blader since
The Birdcage was in limited release.

113.

You can watch *Alice in Wonderland*
or *Mary Poppins*.
It's an Ed Wynn-Wynn situation.

114.

I'm a Pesci-tarian;
I can only eat while watching Joe Pesci movies.

115.

For the record, *The Neverending Story* is an hour
and thirty-four minutes long.

116.

Disney™ created an entire generation unable
to trust Jeremy Irons.

117.

It's cloudy with a chance of meatballs.
(It's overcast, and I'm probably gonna
watch *Meatballs*.)

118.

How did The Three Stooges keep
convincing employers to hire them?
Were their references *ever* checked?

119.

I'd kill to watch a buddy comedy with
Dr. Ruth and Ruth Bader Ginsburg:
Squared Ruth perhaps?

120.

I think the *Fast and the Furious* writers heard,
"Just cut to the chase," once too often
in pitch meetings.

121.

With no vital signs,
vampire checkups are a breeze.
On the other hand, an interview with
one can take hours.

122.

I tried watching that breastfeeding documentary,
but it ended up formulaic.

123.

The White Rabbit has,
"no time to say hello, goodbye,
he's late, he's late, he's late!"
Yet he has time to say all that.

124.

Not many people know this,
but *Beauty and the Beast's* working title
was *Saved by the Belle*.

125.

Brokeback Mountain is two hours of the audience
internally shouting, "But they love each other!"

126.

Everything I know about acting I learned from
Don Knotts, which is telling.

127.

The mirror has two faces.
Especially when twins look in it.

Chapter 4
The Animal Kingdom

128.

If I were a zoologist, I don't think I'd be able to choose just one significant otter.

129.

Everyone loves beef so tender
it falls right off the bone.
Unless the cow is still alive.

130.

That hit the Spot.
So I called the ASPCA.

131.

Dieting dogs only eat abridged homework.

132.

I'm down to my birth weight!
(If I were a Sumatran Rhinoceros.)

133.

A cat family is only as strong as its weakest lynx.

134.

When I feel down, the goose gets angry.

135.

A bear looks snatched after hibernation.

136.

It's a lot less painful to get a camel through the
eye of a needle than the other way 'round.

137.

Every dog has his day,
but in dog years, he has his week.

138.

I'm all for cosmetics testing on animals.
Ugly pets want to be pretty too.

139.

Moth: I Can't Believe it's Not Butterfly.

140.

I don't care how good of friends we are,
if you feed your cat out of a crystal goblet,
we're through.

141.

I just saw a commercial in Sydney with a dog's
voiceover dubbed in, and I said out loud,
"Huh. Even the dogs have Australian accents."

142.

Birds of a feather stick together;
Krazy Glue® works too.

143.

I would not want to be a fly on the wall when the
flyswatter was invented.

144.

Honey *can't* be that high in calories.
Bees are crazy skinny.

145.

Snails are lazy.
They have no get-up-and-escargot.

146.
Don't count your chickens before they hatch.
Especially if they're hard-boiled.
You're setting yourself up for disappointment.

147.
We may not agree on climate change or
evolution, but can we all agree that Dachshunds
mixed with anything else look CA-RAZY?!

148.
"I like bug bits, and I cannot lie."
—   Kermit the Frog

149.
Don't play Koi with me, Goldfish.

150.
Well, the cat's out of the bag:
I need to buy a more secure bag.

151.
What sound do crickets make when they
find something un-funny?

152.

Shoe shopping is the worst part
of parenting an octopus.
Piano recitals are the best part.

153.

Why is everyone so concerned with how much
wood the woodchuck can chuck?
We don't even know, for sure, if he can!

154.

I wanted to adopt this white dog,
but I wouldn't be able to part with her on
Labor Day.

155.

Sure.
Kill two birds with one stone,
and you're *resourceful*.
Kill one bird with two stones,
and PETA is all over you.

156.

Is there anything cuter than a basket of kittens?
Especially if they're all alive.

157.

Mouse and muse are only one letter apart.
Maybe Walt Disney just got confused?

158.

"I've been working on my beached body."
— Shamu

159.

African Elephants are very self-conscious of
their ears while travelling in Asia.

160.

If we don't stop over-fishing,
tuna will be so rare it will only be served Tartare.

161.

A cow once saved my life.
It was bovine intervention.

162.

If I had a petting zoo,
I'd only charge a dollar to pet the llamas.
And I'd call them *The Dollar Llamas*.

163.

"Yo quiero Taco Bell®," loosely translates to,
"Get that Chihuahua away from my Taco Bell®.
That's disgusting!"

164.

"Can we talk about the elephant in the room?"
— Dumbo's parents

165.

If it looks like a duck, swims like a duck,
and quacks like a duck – eat it.
Because duck is delicious.

166.

I want to breed goldfish with elephants:
An animal that can't remember what
it never forgot.

167.

It's a nightmare finding toys for baby boa
constrictors with pieces they can't swallow.

Chapter 5
Observations

168.

If we spent half the time solving
the world's problems that we spend
'Re-imagining Disney Princesses', we'd be set.

169.

Little known fact:
Happy Hour is the euphemism for the
seventh dwarf's *alone time*.

170.

Very few hipster boys actually have hips.

171.

If life is just a bowl of cherries,
there are going to be a lot of disappointed gurus.

172.

A plumber has the shittiest job.

173.

Some days you're Baby Jessica;
Some days you're the well.

174.

Statistically, there *must* be a serial killer with
impeccable hand-writing.

175.

I don't have the official figures in front of me,
but doing an internship is like ten times better
than doing an internment.

176.

You see a lot of new faces on the Upper East Side.
And I mean *new* faces.

177.

For 17 percent of the world's population,
every summer is an Indian summer.

178.

A diorama competition beats a diarrhea
competition any day of the week.

179.

We can put a man on the moon, but we can't make it look like they're actually driving a car on a sitcom.

180.

Europeans:
Give 'em an inch,
and they'll take 2.54 centimeters.

181.

If Garfield found a diner with a lasagna special on Mondays, maybe he wouldn't hate them so much.

182.

Anatomy professors cannot run for President. There are too many skeletons in their closets.

183.

When your bologna has a first name,
you need to get out more.

184.

Cher raised her first-born pro-Bono.

185.

Identity theft is the sincerest form of flattery.

186.

Anise Liqueur sounds more like a drag queen than a beverage.

187.

Most people don't know this,
but on the weekends, Frida Kahlo donated eyebrows to the less fortunate.

188.

Infomercial producers have greatly overestimated our national need to cut pennies in half.

189.

A Madam is a Call Girl with ambition and a ten-year plan.

190.

Breakfast in bed = great!
Breakfast in bedpan = less great.

191.

Celebrity wedding photos, with the groom kissing
the bride's cheek while the bride stares at the
camera, are destroying the fiber of America.

192.

In tennis – Love is nothing.
In life – Love is everything.
For Frances Bean – Love is Mom.

193.

It may not be as cheap as paper towels,
but cocaine is definitely the
quicker picker-upper.

194.

A sunny sky can brighten your day.
Truly.

195.

Rip Torn wins the prize for most
redundant name.

196.

Men are from Mars; Flytraps are from Venus.

197.
"I read a headline..." is the new "I read an article..."

198.
When Arabic lessons are mistaken
for Aerobic lessons,
both parties are confused and disappointed.

199.
That guy's so homophobic,
he never coughs with his head turned.

200.
If you learned Chinese from fortune cookies,
you'd speak only in nouns.

201.
Outside the Box = Good name for a toy store!
Outside the Box = Bad name for an obstetrician's
office.

202.
Presentation is nine-tenths of the law.

203.

I always think we're more alike than different.
Then I see someone buying Strawberry-Kiwi
Juice and realize how wrong I've been.

204.

Disasters are notoriously thorough.
You never hear of an incomplete one.

205.

If a psychic teamed up with an optometrist,
they would have a monopoly on
seeing into the future.

206.

Anyone who says, "You can't have
your cake and eat it too,"
just ran out of the cake they were serving.

207.

You're not officially an adult until you find
yourself telling a fifteen minute story,
the moral of which is,
"Drivers should use their damn turn signals!"

208.

Sadly, *symmetry* isn't a palindrome.
Neither is *palindrome.*

209.

You only live once, unless you're a cat.
Or Shirley MacLaine.

210.

Some families pronounce it *Aunt,*
and some say *Ant.*
It's all relative.

211.

We may speak 6500 different languages,
but looking irritated and tapping your wrist
means '*hurry up*' in every one of them.

212.

If Annie Sullivan were alive today,
she'd be one hell of a *Miracle Twerker.*

213.
Stocks:
If they ain't brokered, don't fix 'em.

214.

Whoever said,
"Good things come to those who wait,"
never waited tables.

215.

Lock someone *out*, and you're fine.
Lock someone *in*, and you're a felon.

216.

They say you can cure allergies with local honey,
but it's just an old hive's tale.

Chapter 6
Technology & Gadgets

217.

In 2005 I joined ChristianMingle® because I thought it was a site to meet guys named Christian.

218.

Adobe® asks me for more updates than my mother.

219.

Nothing defines the *Me Generation* better than Wikipedia.
(They actually have the definition.)

220.

How many domains were suggested before settling on *farmersonly.com*?

221.

Pirates call it a MePhone.

222.

Some plants *hate* Instagram because they are
un-photosynthetic.

223.

The apple didn't fall far from the tree.
Thank God I got the AppleCare®.

224.

Helvetica and I are not compatible.
She's just not my type-set.
But Comic Sans is always good for a laugh.

225.

An app a day keeps productivity away.

226.

Facebook® is a powerful medium:
Third World countries have
overthrown dictators.
We got Betty White on SNL.

227.

Does anyone still Windows® shop,
or are we all Mac® people now?

228.

I caution my friends against using OKCupid™.
If you're going to employ a Cupid,
find one better than just *OK*.

229.

My patience can be summed up thusly:
"Your video will play after the following ad."
NEXT!

230.

The closest I ever come to playing a video game
is watching the Uber drivers get closer.

231.

If you don't want a Trojan virus,
don't look a GIF horse in the mouth.

232.

I didn't read the article on cuticle health.
I just looked at the thumbnail.

233.

I suffer from Pre-Traumatic Post Disorder:
The act of starting to post a comment online
and deciding last minute it's not worth it.

234.

Be warned:
Charlotte's Website has nothing to do with
charming spiders or pigs.
Well, maybe pigs.

235.

Psychics save a bundle on caller ID.

236.

I'm not convinced *FarmVille* is what Al Gore had
in mind when he invented the Internet.

237.

I hope having a child isn't like having Instagram,
where one day I realize I haven't checked
on it in 6 months.

238.

WebMD is a *Chose Your Own Adventure*® book,
with every page leading to imminent death.

239.

I want an eye-rolling app.
These eyes are worn out.

240.

I desperately hope, somewhere in rural America,
there's a ride-sharing app for sheep:
Eweber™.

241.

I've never met anyone with enough to say
that '*ur*' was a necessary abbreviation.

242.

If '*What If?*' had a Wikipedia page,
Brian Dunkleman would take up the first
three paragraphs.

243.

There is nothing worse, in a first world country,
than texting a question mark when you meant
an exclamation point.
"You look great?"

244.

I tried to text a friend, "same here,"
but really sent, "dame here."
Luckily, Maggie Smith was at the door,
so it all worked out.

245.

David Before the Dentist is the prequel we've all
been waiting for.

246.

I would enjoy LinkedIn more if it were a
sausage-of-the-month club.

247.

If I checked my mailbox as often
as I checked my email,
my neighbors would have me committed.

248.

You have to be careful with autocorrect:
Drunk in a ditch and *Drunk in a Dutch*
are two very different things.

249.

We must finally band together and
face the true injustice of our time:
no italics feature on Facebook®.

250.

If a video link says,
"You won't believe what happens next,"
chances are I'll probably believe it.

251.
Which came first:
the asshole or the online comment section?

Chapter 7
Childhood

252.

On the Upper East Side, you can't spell *childhood* without an '*O*' pair.

253.

I wonder if Big Bird is uncomfortable eating Sesame Chicken.

254.

I didn't have a lemonade stand. I had a cheese booth called *Aaaaahhhh, Real Muensters!*

255.

It's unfair that kids can't drink. So few would be here without alcohol in the first place.

256.

As a child, *social media* was my imaginary friend and me co-anchoring our morning news program.

257.

The upside to missing children is it gives
Nancy Grace something to do.

258.

In March I'll be hosting a *Tori Spelling Bee*,
just for girls named *Tori*.

259.

I can't see Smokey the Bear
without feeling guilty.
I've never prevented a forest fire and only *I* can!

260.

When I was little, I wanted to be a serf.
It was feudal.

261.

Battleship is 45 minutes of, *"No, no, no, no,"*
and a lifetime of resentment.

262.

I never played house.
I played *domestic partners*.

263.

The 90's were confusing.
Between *Just Do It* and *Just Say No*,
I'm surprised I *ever* lost my virginity.

264.

My prayer at age 5:
Now I lay me down to sleep...

My prayer at age 35:
Dear Lord, please don't let me
swallow my retainer tonight...

265.

Face puberty like a man, and grow a pair.

266.

"Elmer's®. 2001. Nice body. Robust bouquet.
An excellent year."
       —   Manhattan Preschooler
in Time Out

267.

Comedy comes in threes.
You can imagine my disappointment when I was
born second.

268.
Children's Book Idea:
A coroner with a phonetics disorder,
who literally can't pronounce people dead.

269.
Heartening Proverb:
It takes a village to raise a child.

Disheartening Proverb:
It takes a village to raze a child.

270.
Goats:
The first Garbage Pail Kids.

271.
I can't wait for *Thomas the Tanked Engine –
The College Years.*

272.
I wish my origin story were more interesting,
but really it's just drinking Yoo-hoo® and hanging
out with the adults at family parties.

273.

As a child, I refused to say, "goo-goo, ga-ga."
I found it redundant.

274.

I wish anything excited me now as much as
Bubblicious® did when I was 8.

275.

I was so pretentious as a child,
I had an Easy Bake *Double* Oven.

276.

As a youth, after a bad dream,
I would sing the *My Little Pony*™ themesong.
As an adult, I just sing it an octave lower.

Chapter 8
Literature

277.

I'm fairly sure my cause of death will be exposure
to *The Elements of Style.*

278.

If you give a mouse a cookie and he asks for milk,
set a trap.
Take care of that ungrateful bastard
once and for all.

279.

Curiosity killed the cat,
but it made the monkey an international
literary star.

280.

You're so vain, you probably think your
biography's about you. Don't you? Don't you??

281.

After 20 million copies are sold,
you can stop calling it *The Secret.*

282.

I started Hemingway's, "The Three-Day Blow,"
but I couldn't get into it.
Shocking, I know.

283.

The parents are darn lucky neighbors never
called CPS on Amelia Bedelia.

284.

Cyclops is an optical allusion.

285.

My metaphor is like a simile.

286.

Ok, I admit it: I read Playboy™.
But just for the pictures!

287.

Murder on the Orient Express spoiler alert:
They *all* did it.
(I meant to mention this in 1934.)

288.

I just don't see *The Hunger Games* catching fire.

289.

I'm a little more Nancy than Drew.

290.

I can't believe *O Magazine* is 15 years old!
It seems like just yesterday Oprah appeared on
the cover of ever issue.

291.

I'm not saying a prayer for Owen if he's
such a meany.

292.

"Your body of work is a wonderland."
—   Macmillan & Company to
Lewis Carol, 1865

293.

Goldilocks and the Three Beers is a
much different fairy tale.
Proofreading matters.

294.

I was going to write my memoirs,
but *Ramona Quimby, Age 8* pretty much
covers it.

295.

The Secret Life of Bees?
What do they have to hide??

296.

I'd rather read *The 5 People You <u>Won't</u> Meet in
Heaven*, so I could really focus on getting to know
them before it's too late.

297.

"Chicken Strips."
Menu item?
Or provocative *Farmer's Almanac* headline?

298.

I'm not sure my ninth grade English teacher was
state-certified. We read, *The Mediocre Gatsby,
The Burgundy Letter*, and *To Kill a Ring-necked
Pheasant* – a guide to migratory game birds
of the Northwest.

299.

C'mon *How Now Brown Cow*, don't be assonance.

300.

Elf on the Shelf ends much more happily than
Shelf on the Elf.

301.

Sometimes the plot thickens.
And sometimes, you just reduce the plot on a
low simmer.

302.

If the birds had been gluten-free,
Hansel and Gretel would have been a helluva
lot shorter.

303.

I imagine Bob Cratchit didn't use the phrases
'crippling debt' or *'doesn't have a leg to stand on'*
around Tiny Tim.

304.

I would not, could not in a box.
I would not, could not with a fox.
So please stop asking, Mr. Fox!

305.
"It was a marriage of convenience,
with an emphasis on *con*."
— 1st line of the novel
I'm not writing

306.
"In a world of eye-candy she was a
well-balanced meal."
— 1st line of the 2nd novel
I'm not writing

307.
HAIKU (A Haiku)
A haiku is hard.
Counting syllables and lines.
Screw it. This one's done.

308.
At least four times, in most Dan Brown novels,
a chapter ends with,
"Robert, we've got a problem."

309.
It's a shame they clear-cut the Hundred Acre
Wood to put in that CVS®.

Chapter 9
Holidays &
Celebrations

310.
Oktoberfest is the *wurst* fest.

311.
The rule *Never Wear White After Labor Day*
is just an Urban Outfitter's Legend.

312.
I'm throwing a February surprise party.
The surprise is everyone has to say the first '*R*'
in '*February*'. And in '*surprise*'.

313.
Fat Tuesday:
If Jesus sees his shadow,
it's six more weeks of eating.

314.
And if the groundhog sings "Me and My Shadow,"
it's six more weeks of homosexuality.

315.

Dear Rudolph,
It gets better.
Seasons Greetings,
Kasey

316.

A guy buying a lot of ice for Labor Day looks the
same as a guy buying a lot of ice to bathe you in
after stealing your kidney.

317.

I tried to form a carol group for Christmas,
but I only know 2 ladies named Carol.

318.

Turkeys celebrate Memorial Day on the
4th Thursday in November.

319.

I can't believe it's NASCAR® season already.
I feel like I was *just* taking down the
decorations from last year.

320.

Beware the Ides of March Madness.

321.

Angels make snow-humans in the winter,
and it's as creepy as it sounds.

322.

I dare you to find a better Christmas lyric than,
"the logs on the fire fill me with desire."

323.

Goldfish get to celebrate #ThrowbackThursday
every day.

324.

My hotel is filled with
couples for Valentine's night.
I'm alone in my room watching
Sex Sent Me to the ER, so it's all good.

325.

If Chuck Norris were Santa,
he'd check his list *once*.

326.

My bodega is selling Easter candy.
I'm honestly not sure if it's 6 months early
or 6 months late.

327.

I just saw *The Camryn Manheim
Steamroller Christmas Spectacular*.
I *have* to read the tickets more closely next time.

328.

If I have any more holiday cheer,
I'll get alcohol poisoning.

329.

I'm dreaming of a white Christmas,
but a black Santa because I'm fair and balanced.

330.

I'm so late to the party,
I'm not even sure there was one.

331.

I gave up belly buttons for lint.

332.

I need a little Christmas,
right this very minute.
Candles in the window,
but *no* Carol at the spinet.
She's tone-deaf with two left hands.

333.
Everyone thought I was
dressed as a spider for Halloween,
but *clearly* I was a web developer.

334.
Christmas leftovers:
the calories that keep on giving.

335.
I miss pre-2010 Thanksgivings,
before everyone discovered turkey brining.
And Instagram.

336.
Snow after Christmas is like previews
after the movie.

337.
You know what no one tells you as a kid?
A Christmas Carol is all a bad dream, and Bob
Cratchit wakes, with a start, sitting at his desk
on Christmas Day.

338.
I've never celebrated Precedent's Day,
but there's a first time for everything.

Chapter 10
Planes, Trains, & Automobiles

339.
If *Lord of the Flies* had been set in an airport,
it would have been fifteen pages – max.
(And it would have been a bloodbath.)

340.
It's fitting that Newark's airport code
starts with *EW*.

341.
There's a Finn line between Sweden and Russia.

342.
God bless the emergency exit row;
A crew of six perfect strangers, with thirty-five
seconds of training, assuages any flying
fears I may have had.

343.
My flight attendant was a regular Chatty Cathay.

344.

My dad legitimately thinks the GPS tries to trick
us, and it's our job to figure out the clues.

345.

When it comes to Capitalism,
all roads lead to the Ayn Rand McNally Atlas.

346.

*(On the phone in Toronto, after leaving my
wallet at the Newark Airport)*
REPRESENTATIVE: All you'll need to do, is have
a friend go to Newark and pick it up.
KASEY: I'll just start a new life in Canada,
because _that_ will never happen.

347.

What happens in Vegas stays in Vegas.
Except VD, which can travel.

348.

I don't fret much about my plane going down,
though I would hate for my last meal to be from
Chili'sToo®.

349.
Kissimmee, FL is the most
desperate-sounding city.

350.
Why are airlines still using the equipment I made
Printshop™ banners with in 1992?

351.
When I fly coach,
I pretend it's First Class with appallingly
bad service.

352.
JAPAN, 1600s (A Haiku)
Try to remember
The kind of September when
Haikus were the rage.

353.
Communicating with airline representatives is as
easy as, "Alpha Bravo Charlie."

354.
Cleveland's waterfront at night is Eerie!

355.

The GPS woman, nagging me with the same
directions over and over, is the closest I've come
to traditional marriage.

356.

I almost missed the exit for the New Orleans
airport because the sign said:
NO International Airport.

357.

It seems wrong that airplanes can stay aloft,
but I guess it's Wright.

358.

I don't live on the edge,
but I've contemplated getting a time-share there.

359.

You have to love airports:
The only place on earth you can get hard liquor
at 8 AM on a Monday, and no one bats an eye.

360.

If you ask me, First Class is a flight of fancy.

361.

Some airport terminals have world-class cuisine.
Some have an Auntie Anne's® Pretzels
and a vending machine.
(Which just sells iPhones.)

362.

Seattle is the one place you could find a haystack
in a needle.

363.

If you were hit by a bus today you'd never think,
"I wish I'd spent more time working."
Unless you were the bus driver,
in which case it might've saved your life.

364.

If Skymall® has taught me anything,
it's that Americans have an unyielding
dedication to finding new ways to make, gift,
and drink alcohol.

365.

When I look at a map it always says,
You Ate Here.

366.

Riding New Jersey Transit is like losing
Rock-Paper-Scissors over and over for 2 hours.

Chapter 11
Quack Quotes

367.

"Talk to the hand!"

– Helen Keller, 1895

368.

"The world is my oyster!"

– A Near-sighted Pearl

369.

"And for my *next* trick..."

– A Magician Prostitute

370.

"Mask for Mask."

– The Phantom's Tinder profile

371.

"I'll be your Ken Doll on the water."

– Malibu Ken, by Mattel®

372.

"It's all about eaves with you."

— A Roofer's Wife

373.

"Reach out and touch someone."

— AT&T, 1979

374.

"Reach out and touch everyone."

— The Catholic Church,
1951-2015

375.

"Reach out and touch *no one.*"

— Hillary Clinton, 1998

376.

I'll never forget the advice Marlee Matlin gave me:

"   ."

377.

"When one door closes another one opens."

— Revolving Door slogan,
since 1888

378.
"I would kick him out of bed for eating crackers."
— Gluten-free Slut

379.
"And sometimes when we touch,
the honesty's too much."
— Mary Todd Lincoln in
couples counseling

380.
"I didn't come here to lose."
— Every Reality Show Contestant,
moments before losing

381.
"Who's got one thumb and loves wood shop?
This guy!"
— Most Woodshop Teachers

382.
"Shoe you AND the horse you rode in on."
— Blacksmith, 1802

383.

"I can *handle* this!"
— An Enthusiastic
Doorknob Installer

384.

'I come from good stalk."
— Celery

385.

"I left my heart in San Francisco.
But where did I leave my lungs?"
— Frankenstein

386.

"I put my pants on 8 legs at a time,
like everybody else."
— A Very Down-to-earth Octopus

387.

"My business begins where your business ends."
— Proctologist's Motto

388.

"This too shall pass."
— My Kidney Stone

389.

"Are you a good witch or a bad witch?"
— Glinda, 5 seconds before
telling Dorothy, "Only bad
witches are ugly."

390.

"It's like I'm losing my mime."
— Marcel Marceau's Mother
on his wedding day

391.

"I have a dream!"
— Dr. King

392.

"I had a dream!"
— Mama Rose

393.

"I had a dream, but I can't remember it!"
— Kasey RT Graham

394.

"Look ma! No hands!"
— Armless Mama's Boy

395.

"You don't own me.
I'm not just one of your many toys!"
— Raggedy Ann after
two Apple-tinis

396.

"I need to get back in touch with playing straight.
It's been too long."
— My Husband

397.

"Who the hell invited Y?!"
— The Vowels, sometimes

Chapter 12
Health, Sports, & Fitness

398.
I couldn't be a referee.
I never think there are too many men
on the field.

399.
Have you ever had that moment when you
realize you're the only person you know *not*
teaching a SoulCycle class?

400.
Of course the first pro boxer to come out was
a featherweight.

401.
In my gym pep talks, I call myself *a pansy-ass
candy-striper* more times than I care to admit.

402.

I give my best running commentary
on a treadmill.

403.

Pelé was the original kick-starter.

404.

I want to open a classy sports bar called
Martini Navratilova's.

405.

When your quarterback is injured,
just put in 5 Nickelbacks.

406.

I'm in a two-step program for dance-a-holics.

407.

Ugh.
I have a great boxing joke,
but I can't remember the punchline.

408.

My gym has a little more cake than beef.

409.

Fine!
I *guess* I'll get a chiropractic adjustment.
Twist my arm.

410.

Quite a few football players stretch the limits
and patience of spandex.

411.

"I couldn't have putt it better myself."
— Phil Mickelson

412.

I cycle my workouts every three days:
Head, Shoulders, Knees and Toes.

413.

Can an outfielder nab more than twenty-one pop
flies, or is it a catch 22?

414.
If I got a facelift,
It would certainly raise a few eyebrows.

415.
I love to jump on someone else's treadmill and
chase them.

416.
"This ain't my first rodeo."
—   Second-time rodeo-goer

417.
It's like I told LeBron James at Williams-Sonoma®,
"If you can't stand the kitchen,
get out of the HEAT."

418.
The Raw Diet is excellent for weight loss.
Especially if you start with chicken.

419.
I like my massage like my dough:
gently kneaded by an Italian guy and followed
immediately by a pizza.

420.

I work out because it's only a stone's throw from
David to Goliath.

421.

I wish LMAO were a legitimate weight-loss
technique.

422.

Heading to the gym to say, "Yes to the press!"

423.

My favorite part of a boxing match is when they
stare at each other like they're about to kiss in a
romantic comedy.

424.

I signed up for lasso lessons,
but the instructor threw me for a loop.

425.

We never seem to mind immigrants if they're
playing baseball or basketball.

Chapter 13
Kasey & Ian:
An Imperfect Union

426.

Love is about compromise.
Our wedding vows were, "You'll do."

427.

I hope when Ian is 90, he enjoys
naps as much as I do.
And also, that I'm still alive.

428.

When Ian is sleeping, I walk around like a cat.
(Not quietly. I just lick myself and look for yarn.)

429.

Ian won't let me pick out the Calamine lotion.
He doesn't want me making rash decisions.

430.

I prayed for the Lord to send me patience,
but I was sent Ian instead.

431.

I'm so embarrassed about being clumsy,
when I fall down the stairs, I just say Ian hit me.

432.

I don't shop with children for fear
they'll break everything.
I don't shop with my husband for fear
he'll *buy* everything.

433.

I've never listened to Adele.
Do I need to break up with Ian first,
or can I enjoy the albums on their own?

434.

You have to hand it to Ian.
Correction:
I meant *backhand* it to him.

435.

Does it count as a sex dream if *Dream Ian* just
says, "Get off me, I'm watching *Letterman*"?

436.

Anywhere I hang my husband is home.

437.

When I'm alone and a commercial Ian hates
comes on, I mute the TV, because that's love.

438.

The devil is in the details.
Thankfully, I canceled Ian's subscription
to *Details.*

439.

I told Ian I thought we could move to Portland
one day, which led to a ten-minute argument
about whether or not he'd look good
with a mustache.

440.

Ian and I are watching *Auntie Mame,*
otherwise known as *How to Raise a Homosexual.*

441.

When Ian describes a bad day, it sounds like the
plot of a good Mary Kate and Ashley Olson movie.

442.

Our wedding was so gay, they threw *brown* rice.

443.

I just learned that in 5th grade, Ian listed
Philadelphia as his favorite film on a
Secret Santa form.
(5th grade...)

444.

I don't believe in fairies, but I do believe in Ian.
I clap my hands every morning to wake him up.

445.

I think Ian would be less upset if I left him,
than if he knew I use his Aveda™ shampoo
as body wash.

446.

If Ian and I had a reality show,
it would be like *Punch and Judy*,
but without puppets and *with* homosexuals.
(Ok, *maybe* there'd be puppets.)

447.

Some people give Ian too much credit.
And by people, I mean Visa®, Discover®,
and American Express®.

448.

Being with Ian is great for my
respiratory system.
I take several deep, calming breaths before
responding to anything he says or does.

449.

You can't be held accountable for
killing your husband, right?
Something about spousal privilege?

450.

When Ian and I peruse the celeb-ridden pages of
People™ magazine, we sound like
a pair of spinster owls.
Who? Who???

451.

I'm worried my husband has latent
homosexual tendencies.
Sorry. I meant *blatant.*

452.

When arguing with Ian, I constantly find myself
yelling, "Objection! Relevance, your Honor?"

453.

"I'm a good husband like Macaulay Culkin was
The Good Son."

—   Ian Liberto

454.

I consistently find myself outside fitting
rooms asking women,
"Do you have this much trouble with
your husbands?"

455.

I had a 4-week out written into my
wedding vows.

456.

I try to do a lot of little things that will annoy Ian
now but that he'll recall fondly in my eulogy.

Chapter 14
Advice & Inspiration

457.
Life is a terminal illness.
Accept that, and enjoy the ride.

458.
Decorating rule of thumb:
Spare the rod; spoil the curtains.

459.
"Better lederhosen than neverhosen."
— Bavarian Proverb

460.
Grab life by the balls.
It's more socially acceptable than grabbing
Leif by the balls.

461.
If you put all your eggs in one basket,
be sure it's in the refrigerator.
No one needs a basket of Salmonella.

462.

If it goes without saying, don't say it.

463.

Find a penny pick it up,
then all day you'll have something that
doesn't rhyme with '*up*'.

464.

My motto has always been:
Eat like no one is watching.

465.

Live by the Muppet code:
great friends, running gags,
and plenty of guest stars.

466.

Treat sex and marriage like
avocados and guacamole:
You wouldn't commit to guacamole without
thoroughly inspecting the avocados.

467.

Be the nutcracker, not the nut.

468.

People with glass eyes shouldn't throw stones.

469.

Respect your elders:
Watch *The Golden Girls.*

470.

Don't fret *a plague on both your houses*.
It means you have at least two houses.

471.

A wish for my friends:
May your careers be as long as the song
"American Pie" feels.

472.

It's better to be a day late than a dollar short.
At least then you have a whole day to
come up with the dollar.

473.

Make a lot of younger friends,
and your funeral will be standing room only.

474.

If the best part of waking up is
Folgers® in your cup,
go back to bed.

475.

Whatever you do, do it with pride.
Unless you're a nun.
Or an antisocial lion.

476.

Never order an infomercial product right away.
If you JUST WAIT,
they'll send you another one for free!

477.

If you want something done right,
you have to lower your standard for *right*.

478.

Give a man a fish, and he eats for a day.
Teach a man to fish, and charge him
$50 for the lesson.

479.

When you're a garbage man, it's essential not to
bring your work home with you.

480.

Never put off until tomorrow what you can
convince your husband to do today.

481.

You can't put a price tag on fame.
Well, Minnie Pearl did, but otherwise you can't.

482.

Don't seat Cleanliness next to Godliness at
a dinner party.
By now they're sick of each other.

483.

Why anyone asks my advice is beyond me.
It's always, "Go for it!", "Why not?", or
"Try the free clinic in Chelsea."

484.

Whatever you do, don't break a two-way mirror.
It's fourteen years of bad luck.

485.
Be careful:
"Kiss me, I'm Irish" can quickly turn into
"Don't kiss me, I'm puking."

486.
An apple a day keeps the doctor away.
Unless you're Snow White.

487.
If you ever feel like you can't bounce back,
remember that Roseanne Barr once sang
the national anthem.

488.
It rubs the lotion on its skin,
or else it'll be dry for the rest of the day.

489.
Dress for the husband you want,
not the husband you have.
That's the expression, right?

490.
Make the story of your life a page-turner.

491.

A fun Monday night game is to think about all the
missed career opportunities over the years,
and then eat a gallon of Rocky Road.

492.

Revenge is a dish best served from the left
and cleared from the right.
A vendetta is no excuse for bad etiquette.

493.

You can pull a rabbit out of a hat at a kid's party,
but pull a hat out of a rabbit, and you're fired!

494.

Never forget:
You can start out as the second half of
DJ Jazzy Jeff & The Fresh Prince
and end up Will Smith.
Dream big.

495.

Reach for the moon.
Even if you miss, you'll grab a few stars as a
constellation prize.

Chapter 15
For the Adults

496.

My science teacher and I had great chemistry.

497.

There are few things in life more amusing than
a *pop-up* ad for Viagra®.

498.

I'm looking for wrong in the love places.

499.

I have to admit it:
Donating sperm takes balls.

500.

Porn: The only career in which the entry-level
position is *'Star'*.
(Insert *'entry-level'* joke.)
(Also insert *'insert'* joke.)

501.

If step one isn't *Cut a hole in a box*,
it doesn't matter what step two is.

502.

I don't want to toot my own horn,
but it's the most sanitary.

503.

WAITRESS: Boneless wings or boned?
KASEY: Boned. I'm always boned.
  (Deathly silence)

504.

I wouldn't call him a whore,
but his favorite color *is* penicillin.

505.

I get nervous dropping the soap in the shower,
even when I'm alone.

506.

I'm *Criminal Intent* in the streets and
SVU in the sheets.

507.

Telegram Sexting was confusing:
I want you <STOP>
Put your hand on my knee <STOP>
Don't stop <STOP>

508.

If I ever perish in a plane crash,
make sure the press runs a flattering photo.
And delete my browser history.

509.

I just peed like a race horse.
(With a small man in Lycra® on my back.)

510.

My investment advisor has an asset I could
bounce a quarter off of.

511.

Porn writers are using a very different thesaurus
than the rest of us.

512.

The breast implant market is a bust.

513.

In the interest of full disclosure,
I'm getting naked.

514.

When she said, "Let's go Dutch,"
I assumed I'd get to stick my finger in a dyke.

515.

Papa Bear's porridge and bed were *too hot*
and *too hard*, respectively.
Just saying.

516.

Some dogs hate wearing bandanas.
But how are other dogs supposed to know
what they're into?

517.

No one wants high-schoolers having sex,
but everyone loves to reminisce nostalgically
about having sex in high school.

518.

Victoria's Secret isn't one anymore.

519.
Nutella® and I are in a committed relationship.
Usually we spoon, but sometimes I just
use my finger.

520.
I caught a news special on *senior sex*.
My eyes were opened.
Then quickly shut.

521.
I was bitterly disappointed to learn that
The 9-Inch Diet is a cookbook.

Chapter 16
Fashion

522.

It's truly impressive how many laces one can buy
on a shoestring budget.

523.

Some days I'm more Kevin Kline underwear than
Calvin Klein® underwear, and that's OK.

524.

If a sailor's eyebrows are perfect
forseven days straight,
it's safe to say it's *On Fleek Week*.

525.

I asked Diane Von Furstenberg
about fall dress trends, but in her usual pattern,
she skirted the issue.

526.

My current wardrobe status is threat level:
Sound of Music – The Poor Didn't Want This One!

527.

Fashion has morphed from *Who are you wearing*
to *What are you wearing*?

528.

An underwear model can never half-ass his job.

529.

"Don't put the Converse® before the
skinny jeans."
        –   Traditional Hipster Adage

530.

I get funny looks in Idaho for wearing a
trunk-cut Speedo®.
I get funny looks on Fire Island for wearing a
trunk-cut Speedo® from *last* season.

531.

Like Paula Poundstone in the 90's,
I play it close to the vest.

532.

The Devil wears Prada.
The Devil's Advocate wears Talbots®.

533.

I wouldn't ask Dr. Huxtable to buy
me a sweater.
Or Bill Cosby to buy me a drink.

534.

Gown by Oscar de la Renta = A-OK Fashion
Gown by Oscar De La Hoya = Fashion TKO

535.

American Apparel® models look like they were
caught at an inopportune moment in 1978.

536.

If I owned a fabric store,
I would stock up on bolts of boyfriend material.

537.

People Print never caught on in the
animal world.

538.

Been there. Done that. Got the T-shirt. Wore it.
Returned it for a smaller size. Cut off the sleeves.
Perfect.

539.

Jennifer Aniston brings photos of *herself* into her haircuts for inspiration.

540.

If you're tired of *Project Runway* reruns, change the Chanel.

541.

I would kill to be legal counsel for Fruit of the Loom®, if only so I could say,
"Let me brief you on the Boxers case."

542.

No one rocks a turtleneck or a top hat like Diane Keaton.

543.

If fake orgasms were like fake Louis Vuitton®, straight men still wouldn't know the difference.

544.

Of all the pants, *fancy* are my favorite.

545.
I wager that the amount of money a guy spends
on a pair of underwear correlates directly to
where he falls on the Kinsey Scale.

546.
I'm wearing Vera Wang at my wedding.
I'll wrap her around my shoulders and carry
her down the aisle.

Chapter 17
Who the Hell is Kasey RT Graham?

547.

On average, women live six years
longer than men.
If I live to be 94, I'm getting a sex change.

548.

I don't want to go to court,
but I'd love a tasteful colored pencil sketch of me
on the witness stand.

549.

I have trust issues.
I mean trust fund issues.
The issue being I don't have one.

550.

I don't mind off-white linoleum. Or even ecru.
But I refuse to walk on eggshell in my own home!

551.

In college, I got a BS in bullshitting.

552.

I was going to party like it was 1999,
but I fell asleep like it was 1989.

553.

I'm not a fan of farm-to-table restaurants.
I prefer a sink somewhere in between there.

554.

I wish you could donate fat like you donate blood.

555.

I'm no doctor, but Irritable Bowel Syndrome and
Restless Leg Syndrome would be the worst
combination of syndromes.

556.

I cannot be the only person who is appalled that a
bag of rubber bands comes with a
press-and-seal closure.

557.

My nieces still occasionally slip up and call me
Aunt Kasey.

558.

Most of my jokes resonate so deeply with the
American public, they get a moment of silence.

559.

I get nervous when drag queens come
off the stage.
Antics!

560.

While I slept, I imagined I'd fixed my leaky sink.
But alas, it was just a pipe dream.

561.

My inner-monologue is on shuffle.

562.

"Is there a car commercial that *isn't* an
advertisement for speeding?" is the
oldest-sounding thing I've
ever said out loud.

563.
I've always been a glass half-full kind of guy,
which is maybe why I'm so dehydrated?

564.
I'd be terrible in war. If a fellow soldier said,
"Leave me! Save yourself," I'd ask,
"Are you sure?", but just once to be polite.

565.
KASEY SAYS: Sure! I can rearrange my plans
and hang out!
KASEY THINKS: I *guess* I can set my crockpot to
low instead of high...

566.
My worst fear is being found dead after a fall in
the shower, and I'm not at my goal weight.

567.
I cry at the drop of a hat.
I just feel terrible for people who drop their hats!

568.
My blind friend and I have a ton of inside jokes,
but they're visual jokes, so don't tell him.

569.

If there's a Living-Anti-Social, sign me up!

570.

I was told today that my sense of humor
is *too corny*, which is alarming.
Corn is high in carbs!

571.

Instead of a firming cream I bought
affirming cream.
It looks at my face and says:
You is smart.
You is kind.
You is important.

572.

I signed up for the Marines.
I ordered two, but they never showed up.

573.

I threw caution to the wind,
and all I got was a face full of caution.

574.

I can't say, "I'm gay," with a straight face.

575.

I'm not scared of becoming an old person.
I've been practicing since I was eleven.

576.

I long for a dramatic business dealing, at which I
could say, "This is a one time offer.
It expires the second I walk out this door.
Think it over."

577.

If you've never purposefully burped
to make room for more eating,
we have nothing left to talk about.

578.

Am I the only New Yorker who felt a pang of
jealousy upon reading, "Boston bombing suspect
living in a 10 foot X 10 foot cell"?

579.

I prefer to do my notary in private, thank you.

580.

I'm going to pull out all the stops and
write a telegram!

581.

It's hard being gay with a good worth ethic:
You work hard, it puts hair on your chest,
and then you have to shave it right off again.

582.

I know an ounce of pretension is worth a
pound of manure, yet I always have to
google lbs to kilos.

583.

I urinate around everything that's mine
in case that trend returns.

584.

I'm not a Renaissance man.
But then, I'm not much for faires in general.

585.

Sometimes I throw myself on the Deli case and
cry, "They were so young!"

586.

I don't repeat jokes. They just go into
syndication.

587.

I don't repeat jokes. They just go into syndication.

588.

I prefer cigars to cigarettes.
I like big butts, and I cannot lie.

589.

Figuratively is literally my favorite word.

590.

I wanted to study musical theatre,
but curiosity killed the *CATS*.

591.

With me, it's not so much about finding my purpose as it is about *funding* my purpose.

592.

I'm sure the hotel maid thinks it's cocaine on the bathroom counter,
but it's most definitely Metamucil®.

593.

My pirate name would be Swish Buckler.

594.

I'm a *Little Orphan Annie* in a *Cathy* world
with *Maxine's* figure.

595.

If Jimmy had cracked a vase,
I might have balked.
But it was just corn. Of course I didn't care.

596.

When I look in a mirror, it's like I'm on
Insta-Graham.

597.

I swear my elevator just told me,
"You're going down."

598.

Just flew in from the gun show,
and boy are my *arms* tired!

599.

When I said I wanted to live in a pre-war building,
I should have specified *which* war.

600.

This? This isn't *my* joke, officer.
I'm just telling it for a friend.

601.

I have an open door policy.
It makes it much easier to get into the room.

602.

I could never name my son Mike for fear I'd drop
him every time I landed a really strong point.

Chapter 18
Food & Drink

603.

I ordered a breadbasket at this Indian
restaurant, but they had naan.

604.

The Titanic incident upsets me so much that I
still can't eat iceberg lettuce.

605.

I see the world through
Rosé-colored glasses.

606.

Boxed cake mixes are gateway recipes.

607.

Chinese food is so good,
every state should be a right to wok state.

608.
You can lead a horse to water,
but you can't make him drink.
Which is why so few horses are in AA.

609.
I don't drink coffee,
and the commercials make me feel I've missed
celebrating all the moments of my life.

610.
Quoth the ravenous, "Always more."

611.
I have won an exorbitant amount of eating
contests in which no one else was aware
of the competition.

612.
I like carbs so much, I would French bread.

613.
My investigation of Idaho found a lot of dirt
on potatoes.

614.
SANGRIA (A Haiku)
Apples float aloft.
Plums drift lazily downward.
White wine in-between.

615.
Is there a more exquisite phrase in the English
language than *All-You-Can-Eat?*

616.
The Sturgeon General warns:
Stop eating fish!

617.
I literally just did a Google™ maps search for
24-Hour Cake.

618.
I'm so passionate about mimosa education,
I'm founding *The Dead Moëts Society.*

619.
I bet that guy thought I was checking him out,
but it was absolutely his ice cream cone.

620.

Of all the alliteration in existence,
personal pan pizza is my favorite.

621.

Dear Olive Garden®,
In a perfect world, I'd never have to choose
between unlimited soup <u>or</u> salad.
Your Obedient Friend,
Kasey

622.

Beef: It's what's for dinner.
Pork: The other white meat.
Tofu: Someone please f***ing eat me.

623.

I have no problem holding my liquor.
It's putting it down that's the hard part!

624.

Drunkenly, I looked at the cab's meter and
thought, "$3.70? Hmm, it seems later."

625.

My Mexican food went south.

626.

What about a French restaurant called
Eateth Pilaf?

627.

I know eighteen Italian words.
All of them are gelato flavors.

628.

I've been yo-yo dieting for years.
Really, once you get past the plastic,
they're not that bad.
Kind of stringy, but otherwise, not bad.

629.

Of all the jokes in the world, my favorite is a
waiter offering a six-ounce pour of wine
when they sell a nine.

630.

I ordered the potato pasta,
and I swear the waitress muttered,
"Oh Gnocchi didn't!"

631.

When it rains, I pour.

632.

"How good does *that* look?"
— Ina Garten, 2002, 2003, 2004...

633.

I spend too much time stewing about tomatoes.

634.

If spoiled milk had a better PR person,
it could be the next Sour Cream!

635.

I tried goofing around with bagels,
but I was never good at roll-play.

636.

My kale chips recipe says, "Perfect for parties
and a great conversation starter,"
which explains why people won't
shut up about kale.

637.

Every night that I don't order
buffalo wings is a win for me.
And for chickens everywhere.

638.

My wedding vow was, "For Better or For Wasted."

639.

I thought I had a fabulous cabbage joke,
but I was just grasping at slaws.

640.

No celebrity makes me hungrier than
Kevin Bacon.

641.

Except perhaps Jon Hamm.

642.

Or Alyssa Milano.

643.

I found a pastry in Florence that I had to take
around the corner to eat, so we could be alone.

644.

I tried to make a winter vegetable stew,
but there's a leek in my crockpot.

645.

If I owned a restaurant that served neither
Italian food nor chicken,
I'd call it *No Parm/No Fowl.*

646.

It's a mimosa, hold the OJ kind of morning.

647.

There's a white wine I like,
but I'm drawing a blanc.

648.

Serving sizes on bags of chips are adorable.

649.

If I were a gay salad posting a personal ad,
I would insist applicants be mesclun.
Or at least mesclun-acting.

650.

It's 10 PM.
Do you know where your drink is?

651.

I can't get on board with heirloom tomatoes.
I refuse to eat hand-me-downs.

652.

A champagne hangover is BRUTal.

653.

When my cooking seems dated,
I throw in currants.

654.

I ate half of a tres leches cake.
So, I guess I ate a 1.5 leches cake.

655.

When I'm hungry, I order two of everything
and play Noah's Ark.

656.

I don't follow the food pyramid.
I've never enjoyed Egyptian cuisine.

657.
ODE TO SPAM® (A Haiku)
Greasy pork product,
Glist'ning in an oval can.
Monty Python Gold.

658.
Remember when we all discovered
baked brie in 2005?
That was fun.

659.
If you ask me, pretzels are twisted.

660.
Some artists need a patron to get their shot.
This artist needs to get a shot of Patrón.

661.
I can't choose between bananas and ice cream.
I'm split!

662.
I'm the Ansel Adams of taking shots.

663.
Dear Taco Bell®,
Please stop wrapping food in other food.
Best Wishes,
Kasey

664.
I'm a sucker for a lollipop and
a sap for maple syrup.

665.
If we're dealing with hypothetical situations,
I'd rather be stranded on a *Dessert* Island.

666.
I'd hoped to open a breakfast store,
but it's a quiche market.

Chapter 19
Music

667.

Whip your Nae Nae, and everyone loves it.
Whip your Nana, and you're arrested.

668.

Would the Village People have been as successful
if they'd been a Cowboy, a Cop, and
A Dental Hygienist?

669.

I couldn't stay up for the total eclipse last night,
so I listened to my *Best of Bonnie Tyler* album
this morning.

670.

Some rappers have a blatant disregard for
perfect rhymes.

671.

Unfortunately, it was Yolanda Saldívar
who killed the radio star.

672.
Dear Sam Cooke,
Perhaps lead with your strengths
before admitting you don't know much about:
History,
Biology,
A science book,
The French you took,
Geography,
Trigonometry,
Algebra,
What a slide rule is for, etc.
Sincerely Yours,
Kasey

673.

Is it only me who hears
'Blacke Eyed Peas' as *'black guy pees'*?

674.

There's nothing more devastating than being
married to a mariachi band member who works
from home.

675.

Beyoncé drops *Lemonade*,
and people lose their minds.
I drop lemonade,
and the Applebee's™ waitress asks me to leave.

676.

Sometimes you just need to *yield* in the name of love.

677.

I know why the caged bird sings.
It's why he only sings Aaron Neville that I
can't figure out.

678.

"I'm every woman, it's all in me!"
— Sybil Dorsett

679.

Thanks to pop music I never misspell respect,
divorce, or bananas.

680.

Michael Bublé always sounds like he's trying to
have sex with your mother.

681.

"If you're handless and you know it
clap your...oh shit."
— 1st Draft Problems

682.

In high school I started a Barbra-shop quartet.

683.

I accidentally left my milkshake in the yard.
I woke up to a lawn full of boys with diarrhea.

684.

If I had a twin and a drag act, we'd call it:
Cher and Cher Alike.

685.

I'm so out of the loop, I called 50 Cent *Half-Dollar.*

686.

If aliens came to Earth and only found a Kelly
Clarkson album, they would dedicate their
mission to destroying the man who hurt that
poor girl.

687.

There is a direct correlation between the tempo
at which one performs, "Baby, It's Cold Outside,"
and its resemblance to a date rape anthem.

688.

If music really were the food of love,
my piano would be stickier.

689.

I want Smashing Pumpkins, The Red Hot Chili
Peppers, and Korn to play a vegetable medley
together.

690.

I'm hoping Bob Vila, Miley Cyrus, and
Dame Judi Dench come up in the same
conversation, so I can finally break out my
Workbench/Twerk Dench limerick.

691.

You'd never guess it, but I LOVE rap music.
I'm the exception that proves Ja Rule.

692.

Lady Gaga,
Please step back from the edge of glory.
It sounds dangerous.
Thank you.
Kasey

693.

If I were in a female punk rock group,
we'd be 'The Broadband'.

694.

"Oh, I got fronds in low places."
— Garth Brooks, gardening

695.

Until I was 31, I thought Sir Mix-a-Lot was an
English pastry chef.

696.

I will *not* play that funky music,
and STOP CALLING ME *WHITE BOY*!

697.

If my mother had named me Biggie Smalls,
I would be too confused to ever get out of bed.

698.

This man just tripped over a
piece of caution tape.
Now *that's* ironic, Alanis Morissette.

699.
I like classical music,
but sometimes you have to think
outside the Bachs.

700.
I get too hungry for dinner at 8,
but I maintain that I am NOT a tramp.

701.
I have no clue what the VMA's are,
but surely there's a cream for them?

702.
"How Much Is That Window in the Doggie,"
is a much darker song.

703.
I want to do a Yo-Yo Ma photo exhibit:
Cello Shots.

Chapter 20
Product Displacement

704.

I love the new Calvin Klein®
enhancement underwear:
I Can't Believe It's Not Butt™.

705.

Dear Red Lobster®,
You cannot have a *'Lobster-Fest.'*
Your mission statement is *'Lobster-Fest.'*
Regards,
Kasey

706.

Yes, Virginia, there is a Slim.

707.

My Subway Sandwich Artist™ today
was a surrealist.

708.
If you're lactose intolerant,
there's no *right* way to eat a Reese's®.

709.
I lit a Yankee Candle® in Atlanta and was run
out of town.

710.
Smucker's®:
that's my jam.

711.
I was so hip as a toddler,
I could totally pull off Pull-Ups®.

712.
We have an energy crisis,
and I blame Motel 6®.

713.
I assume *Noodles* is the silent partner in
Noodles *&* Company.

714.

I want to market a dirt-cheap spirit called
Absolut Worst Vodka®.

715.

When the Dippin' Dots® stand is closed,
it's sadly the *Ice Cream of the Past*.

716.

If Plan B® is your Plan A,
it's time to re-strategize.

717.

Choosy moms choose Jif®,
but choosy dads choose Jill.
She takes Pilates.

718.

When you find a 2-liter of New Coke®
behind a 6-pack of Crystal Clear Pepsi®,
it's time to clean out the fridge.

719.

Every kiss begins with Kay,
which explains why her entire class had
cold sores.

720.

I would do anything for love,
but I would do more for a Klondike® Bar.

721.

Take Beano® before, and there'll be no gas.
(The same is true for Draino®.)

722.

I'm returning these Oreos.
I was specifically assured that black don't crack.

723.

A beer in the hand is worth two
Anheuser-Busch®.

724.

People crave Dr. Pepper®,
but no one's ever asking for Mr. Pibb®.
Just shows what Med School can do.

725.

Ruby:
It's not just for Tuesdays anymore.

726.

A Trapper Keeper® is the most aggressive
school supply.

727.

I always carry toffee around,
so when times are tough,
at least I have my Heath®.

728.

2012 OVERTURE (A Haiku)

Twinkies® closing down.
Blame the unions or yourself?
You last bought one, when?

729.

I went to the trouble of finding the Hidden Valley®,
and they only had oil and vinegar.

730.

I want to market Clif-hanger Bars.
They're just ¾ of a Clif Bar®.

731.

Etonogestrel has a certain NuvaRing® to it.

732.

I opened Pandora®'s Box,
and all I found was an expensive charm bracelet.

733.

Roger Rabbit made a big splash,
but the Nesquik® Bunny's got staying power.

734.

If Adele had been famous in 2001,
Adele, you're getting a Dell®, could've been the
finest slogan in history.

735.

I'll never get over being older than
MTV® *and* the Dairy Queen® blizzard.

736.

"I'm a catch!"

— Charlie the Tuna

737.

Heinz ventured into the mustard business late,
and it couldn't ketchup.

738.

I still get night terrors from the Skittles®
pox commercials.

739.

Somebody laid a finger on my Butterfinger®
after I specifically said nobody better do it!

740.

My Rite Aid® bag split open,
and Halleluiah it was raining Mentos®!

741.

As I grew up, I realized my toy
brick-building skills weren't top-notch.
It was hard, but I had to Lego® my ego.

742.

I tried following those Progressive® commercials,
but you need a Flo chart!

Chapter 21
Politics

743.
FDR was a huge asset to his water polio team.

744.
We'll cross that bridge when Governor Christie closes it.

745.
Ian and I are basically socialists.
We *love* socializing.

746.
Democrat birds loathe their right wing.

747.
I can't believe the Supreme Court is
hearing oral arguments on marriage equality.
I thought *oral* was the one thing we
could all agree on.

748.

I like my wine pours like my men:
liberal.

749.

If I were the first lady of drag,
I'd be Cockamamie Eisenhower.

750.

The 2012 GOP question du jour:
Would you elect a Mormon?
The 2016 GOP question du jour:
Would you elect a moron?

751.

If men had to have the babies,
not only would abortions be legal,
the clinics would have drive-thrus.

752.

Can Congress please discuss a bailout for
Daylight Savings and Loan?

753.

Primates are split over the ethics of
Plantained Parenthood.

754.

I watched two days of the Republican National
Convention before I realized it wasn't a
Grumpy Old Men marathon on TBS™.

755.

I'm sorry media,
but you CANNOT run the headline,
"Monica Lewinsky finally ready to open up."

756.

Today I believed six impossible things
before breakfast.
They were all on Fox News.

757.

If you're a judge removed from the Atlanta
bench, you're a Georgian impeached.

758.

I don't understand the issue
over two men raising a child.
America had forefathers,
and she's doing just fine.

759.
I don't want to hear one more word about a
female politician's menstrual cycle, period.

760.
I imagine the CNN article entitled,
"How to Watch the Debate Tonight,"
is not about alcohol, antidepressants,
or suicide pacts.

761.
If I were a monarch, my slogan would be,
"Kings Rule!"

762.
When it comes to the environment,
you're either forest or against us.

763.
A Log Cabin Republican makes as much sense
as a deer in the NRA.

764.
The marijuana legalization battle started as
a grassroots movement.

765.

My pop culture references are from the
Roosevelt years.
(Teddy Roosevelt)

Chapter 22
The Burning Questions

766.

Is a hoarder of history an annals retentive?

767.

Why were bulls spending enough time in china shops that they needed their own simile?

768.

If the world is my oyster,
and all the world's a stage,
why aren't there more plays about my oyster?

769.

Isn't it racist to *assume* that a hat dance is Mexican?

770.

Are you still able to rub salt in a wound if you're on a low-sodium diet?

771.

If you make a double entendre in the woods,
and no one is around to say,
"That's what *she* said,"
did you really make a double entendre?

772.

Why buy the cow when everyone is drinking
almond milk anyway?

773.

Do you suppose architects ever suffer
from an Edifice Complex?

774.

When geese get nervous do they just
get...bumps?

775.

What hangover remedy do bald dogs use?

776.

Can you truly expect the unexpected?

777.

Anyone know a store where I can get a
less-sharp image?

778.

Shouldn't sword manufacturers make *all* models
double-edged?

779.

When I have a question, regardless of what it is,
I will *always* ask Sherwin-Williams®.

780.

They say diamonds are forever,
but who can prove it?

781.

Do physics majors torque when they're at a club?

782.

Does a shoe store smell like new shoes,
or do new shoes smell like a shoe store?

783.

What if eHarmony just ended up being a
G♯ and a B?

784.

How do people go to Happy Hour and then
do anything else?

785.

Why do Opera composers kill their heroines with
consumption when coughing is so bad
for the voice?

786.

What do folks who get back into riding a bicycle
compare the ease of the experience to?

787.

If you're over 80 and live in Brooklyn,
are you an artificial hip-ster?

788.

Who's for an Ellen DeGeneres and Rosie O'Donnell
talk-show called *Lesbi-honest*?

789.

Do you ever just get the feeling you have
a sixth sense?

790.

If a picture is worth a thousand words,
why isn't the dictionary just an
illustrated pamphlet?

791.

When did the world decide mustaches on sticks
were the only props needed for a successful
photo booth?

792.

What if it truly were all about that bass?

793.

When will '*Surprise*' be added to the
Periodic Table of Elements?

794.

Do funeral homes have customer
appreciation days?

795.

If you sell a ton of hotcakes,
what do you use as your simile?

Chapter 23
Self-deprecation

796.
I always get the last laugh.
(I'm usually the last one to get the joke.)

797.
I'm so unfashionable,
I couldn't even be an accessory to murder.

798.
I took a *Let's Guess How Old You Are* quiz.
The verdict was:
Dead for Six Months.

799.
I live in a doorman building.
He's a pot dealer, who hangs out on the stoop,
but he *does* sign for packages.

800.
I like myself, but the British version was better.

801.
I just ordered thirty-two pieces of fried chicken
and was asked, "For here, or to go?"

802.
I make my omelets *without* breaking a few eggs.
No one likes my omelets.

803.
When I was single,
my sex-life was like a Magic Eye® picture;
You could stare at it for weeks and
still not see anything.

804.
I'm so cheap,
I'm wearing last season's *look of distain.*

805.
People have been laughing at me my whole life.
I choose to believe it's because *'K'* sounds
are funny.

806.
Sometimes I fear I'm the irrelevance in the room.

807.

I used to think I kind of had
a way with the ladies.
I now realize it was just a lady kind of way.

808.

The neighbors complained about
my singing in the shower.
Maybe it was my volumizing shampoo?

809.

Some days, the realization that my childhood
wasn't f***ed up enough to exploit
for art is devastating.

810.

On the first day of kindergarten,
I brought a bell pepper for the teacher.
It was dark in the pantry.

811.

You say I throw like a girl.
I say, "Girls throw like *me*!"

812.

My metabolism has been freelance for years.

813.

I took an A.D.D. test once,
but then an episode of *Robot Chicken* came on,
and what was I talking about?

814.

Not to brag, but my first Christmas card every
year is always from my dentist.

815.

I tried Snapchat,
but all that snapping hurt my fingers.

816.

I strive to be Flash Gordon,
but I hit closer to Gale Gordon.

817.

Mirror, mirror on the wall, who's the fairest —
WELL AT LEAST LET ME FINISH!

818.

Someone told me I should do stand-up,
but I think they just needed my chair.

819.

In my biopic, I'd like to be played by a
young David Hyde Pierce type,
but I'm pretty sure it will be more of a
mature Doris Roberts type.

820.

My Spanish app repeatedly quizzes me on,
"The cake is _mine_."
I'm trying not to take it personally.

821.

If you look up *'slippery slope'*, it's a picture of me
sitting down to have *'just a few'* bites of ice cream.

822.

I'm so un-hip, I need a pop-and-locksmith.

823.

Most people go through an awkward period.
I went through an awkward exclamation point!

824.

I know comedy.
Not that well, though.
We're just Myspace™ friends, really.

825.

I wish my doctor weighed me on a scale of
one to ten.

826.

I look more photogenic in pictures.

827.

My reputation secedes me.

828.

I'm so far behind the times,
I'm just now smoking *320*.

Chapter 24
Television

829.
Zack and Slater never grasped the
Bros Before Hoes rule.

830.
When watching *The View* at the gym,
I came dangerously close to falling off the
treadmill when Barbara Walters addressed
Whoopi as Oprah.

831.
Until this morning,
I thought *Duck Dynasty* was a remake of *Dynasty*
with the cast of *Duck Tales*.

832.
I desperately want to see an episode of *The
Barefoot Contessa* co-hosted by Animal
from The Muppets.

833.
After *19 Kids*, I'd stop counting.

834.

My barista never spells my name right,
which makes me the star of *Mad About Brew*.

835.

Land a spacecraft on a celestial comet,
and you're a hero.
Land a spacecraft on Comet from *Full House*,
and you're a monster.

836.

How has *Law & Order* never done a
Jeep Strangler episode?

837.

You never forget the day you realize Peter Griffin
and Nanny Fine have the same laugh.

838.

Hue Hefner is a colorful character.

839.

NETFLIX's *'Are You Still Watching'* prompt
might as well say, "Read a book, Loser!"

840.

I pray someday *Chopped* will be able to afford a
second ice cream maker.

841.

Dear TV Cops,
Speaking into your sleeve
never comes off as incognito.
Thank you for your time,
Kasey

842.

What about an HGTV show where gay guys
renovate bathrooms?
Flushing Queens perhaps?

843.

I'm not much for horses on TV,
but *Mister Ed* spoke to me.

844.

I didn't serve in Desert Storm,
but I'm pretty sure *Cupcake Wars* is not an
accurate representation of battle.
Maybe Dessert Storm?

845.

Wake me when they make *NCIS: Des Moines*.

846.

So much of the *60 Minutes* team has passed,
it's going to be *15 Minutes* from now on.

847.

I'm watching Canadian *Chopped*.
So far, the only differences are everyone's polite,
and they don't chop anyone, so as not
to hurt feelings.

848.

Whenever someone asks me, "What time is it?"
I get everyone around to yell, "Tool Time!"

849.

You will Rue McClanahan the day you don't
thank me for being a friend!

850.

Some days I'm filled with boundless optimism,
and some days I see there's a TV show called,
Dog With a Blog.

851.

I don't know how spies can be double
or triple agents.
I have a hard time following an episode of
Malcolm in the Middle.

852.

The saddest thing I've ever heard
on a cooking show is,
"Grandma Nonna...You've been chopped."

853.

Based on the lady next to me at the gym,
a great TV show would be black women watching
The King of Queens and just shaking their heads.

854.

When I get tired and cranky,
I end up speaking in Laura Petrie octaves.

855.

If SVU has taught me anything, it's *don't give a
press conference on the steps of the courthouse.
YOU'RE GONNA GET SHOT!*

856.

The most unrealistic thing about reality TV
is that people answer their phones.

857.

Needing a rhyme for *'girls'* is a terrible reason to
keep the youngest one in curls for five seasons.

858.

How, in a very full house, did Stephanie Tanner
drive a car into the kitchen with *no one* hearing?

859.

I have a Roma Therapy candle.
I can't sleep without the scent of
Touched by An Angel.

860.

I want to take Raven-Symoné to a Starbucks®,
so I can finally say, "That's Soy, Raven!"

861.

By the time I figured out the HIMYM acronym,
the series was over.

862.

I strive to have Jo's grit, Blair's style,
Tootie's innocence, and Natalie's Joi De Vivre.
But really I just have Mrs. Garrett's voice.

863.

My life has so many unanswered questions,
I'm basically a teaser for the next
episode of *SOAP.*

864.

Some people have never seen the
prequel series to *Saved By the Bell.*
To those people, I say, "Ignorance is Miss Bliss."

865.

Mayim Bialik is blossoming on
The Big Bang Theory.

866.

I want to watch *The X-Files,*
but I missed *Files A – W.*

867.

The only skill a reality show host needs is the
ability to count backwards from 10.

868.

It's only a matter of time before
Law & Order: SVU has a "Nobody Puts Baby in
the Coroner's" episode.

869.

My life is like *Will & Grace:*
better in thirty minute increments
and best in the late 90's.

870.

Remember that episode of *Murder, She Wrote*
where Jessica Fletcher visited for the
weekend and no one died?
Me neither.

871.

My mother has decided that the characters on
Frasier are *'too randy'* and wants to know if
there is anything I can do about it.
(It's been off the air for ten years.)

872.

You know you've watched too much Nancy Grace
when you see a couple walking on a bridge,
and your first thought is,
"He's probably tossing her over."

873.

I like the option of watching *The Mickey Mouse Club,* because sometimes you feel like Annette, sometimes you don't.

874.

I can't help it:
If Rocky Mountain oysters are mentioned on The Food Network™, I cross my legs.

875.

I want a theme song for my life,
preferably a long one that can be cut down for later seasons.

876.

Clarissa explained it all,
but I still have questions!

877.

I saw a grown man using a pay phone,
and for a moment,
I thought I'd been Quantum Leaped.

878.

A creative idea for a sitcom would be a husband who's an idiot and his hot wife who does everything right.

879.

A good man is hard to find, but *Big Love* didn't make a great case for the alternative.

880.

If my life were an episode of *FRIENDS*, it would be titled,
"The One About The Dying Cell Phone."

881.

Some people are the Carrie of their group, some are the Samantha.
I'm the Jessica Tandy.

882.

If they ever invent supply closets that don't lock from the inside, sitcoms will be over.

883.

Law and Order: SVU is equal parts sex crimes and waiting for a violin line to resolve.

884.
Dear Sitcoms,
We've exhausted the '*bad date ordering the twenty-minute-to-prepare soufflé*' punch line.
Yours truly,
Kasey

885.
If they add another hour to *The Today Show*,
they'll have to call it *Tomorrow*.

886.
I'm watching *The Real Housewives of Duluth*.
Oh, wait. It's just a re-run of *Hoarders*.
Carry on.

887.
I have a very real fear of dancing that I believe
was caused by the opening credits of
The Cosby Show.

888.
I wish I lived in *Married with Children*,
where literally anything is possible.

889.
I enjoy this soap opera,
but I wish they had set it in a more
specific hospital.

Chapter 25
Religion

890.
We are all God's creatures.
Nuns are his creatures of habit.

891.
New York City in July is enough to make *anyone*
doubt the lyrical promise of "Jesus Loves Me".

892.
When God closes a door,
it's usually because he's tired of hearing
you talk about *The Bachelor*.

893.
"Today is the rest day of the first of my life."
— God, Day 7

894.
My boss is a Karen Carpenter.
That's the saying, isn't it?

895.

My puritanical roots need a touch-up.

896.

"They say practice makes perfect,
but only God makes perfect."
— World's Worst
Piano Teacher

897.

I'll bet a lot of hipsters have
'*Leviticus 19:28*' tattoos.

898.

Noah is my favorite Ark-type.

899.

I'm thinking of joining a more
skeptical enlightenment group:
The Illumi-not-so-fasty.

900.

I finally have a Guttenberg bible!
(Steve Guttenberg's, but it still counts!)

901.
If they served a nice white wine with
communion, I'd go to church more often.

902.
I'm pretty sure Jesus doesn't care for 90% of the
pop music covers of his carols.

903.
Eat every supper like it's your last supper.

904.
Catholics eat fish on Fridays in Lent.
It's good for the heart but bad for the sole.

905.
The Westboro Baptist Church's
color guard team is awful.
Apparently God hates *flags*, too.

906.
I was going to give my piano to a church,
but I'm only registered for organ donation.

907.
I'm not anti-Semitic,
but I could never take my dog to a Dr. Katz.

908.
I don't care if *Jesus* made it himself,
I'm not paying $24 for a glass of wine.

909.
Vacation Bible School:
The original ChristianMingle®.

910.
Every time God closes a door,
he opens the Windex®.
He's a clean freak.

911.
Chanting can be a little one-note.

Chapter 26
Absurdities

912.

For a pessimistic proctologist,
life is just a bowel of cherries.

913.

My mouth is an open book.

914.

It's such a sad story about that
comedian who slipped on the banana peel;
The doctors say he'll never be funny again.

915.

If I've said it once,
I've said it a thousand times.
And I probably have,
because *'it'* is one of the most common words.

916.

In my next life,
I want to believe in reincarnation.

917.

Order the blue plate special in the red light
district, and your meal ends up purple.

918.

You're only as old as you feel,
so I'll meet you at IHOP® at 4:30pm for dinner?

919.

Molehills get a bad rap.
I'm sure many are worthy of being made
into mountains.

920.

I'm gonna go out on a limb here,
which is a daring 'cuz I'm afraid of heights.

921.

If I could have dinner with any celebrity from the
past, I'd kill Tina Fey and have dinner with her.

922.

It breaks my heart:
Michelangelo had to paint the ceiling white again
before he could get back his deposit.

923.

I hate public displays of affectation.

924.
<u>LAUNDRY DAY (A Haiku)</u>
Lost sock in dryer.
Throw it out _then_ find the match.
Vicious spin cycle.

925.

If there is one thing I hate most – it's prioritizing.

926.

I was recently asked, completely seriously,
"You went to Penn State, right? Is that in Ohio?"

927.
I just used a mall toilet that
thought it was a bidet.
The worst part?
It was a urinal.

928.
Nurples come in no other colors,
so the _'purple'_ is superfluous.

929.
After watching *Saw* must you to call it *Seen*?

930.
This 1.5 million dollar apartment is giving me
ARCHETECTURAL In-DIGESTion.

931.
Times are tough.
The Witness Protection Program is now just
camouflage Snuggies®.

932.
The little piggy who went to market was severely
traumatized by the *bacon* section.

933.
"The shingles virus is already inside you,"
is the anatomical equivalent of,
"The call is coming from inside the house."

934.
I'm going to take this 10K in stride,
which is a big step!

935.

If the entirety of one's fowl are feuding you can honestly say, "All my ducks are in a *row*."

936.

I thought I could hack it as a graffiti artist, but the writing's on the wall.

937.

If I were a graffiti artist, my tag would be: Spray it, don't say it.

938.

Why do I spend so much time thinking about graffiti artists?

939.

I learned the hard way, you're supposed to *slice* the cucumbers before putting them on your eyes.

940.

I accept that birds do it. And bees do it.
However, I refuse to accept that
educated fleas do it.
For starters, where'd they get this education?
Most join the circus.

941.
If my Art of Suspense class has
taught me anything, it's –

Chapter 27
Theatre

942.

The saddest part of a middle school production of
Romeo and Juliet, is the life-long scar inflicted on
the girl playing the Nurse.

943.

I was pleasantly surprised to learn that
Sondheim on Sondheim is not,
in fact, an adult film.

944.

I'm producing a musical about a dancer
with low self-esteem:
Can't-Can't.

945.

My hotel is hosting a women's
bowling convention.
I haven't seen this many ladies with balls
Since the *La Cage* auditions.

946.

I've finally found a mash-up NO ONE wants to see:
Fifty Shades of Grey Gardens.

947.

Spoiler alert:
Hamilton ends up on the ten-dollar bill.

948.

For pretty much three decades,
I assumed *'doing lines in the bathroom'* was a
rehearsal memorization technique.

949.

When Idina Menzel drops an apple,
she's justifying gravity.

950.

"That bald cap is totally convincing!"
  — No Community Theatre Director
       of *Annie* ever.

951.

"That bald cap is totally convincing!"
  — No Community Theatre Director
       of *The King and I* ever.

952.
"Don't do anything until something makes you."
— Sanford Meisner
(Great rule for acting.)
(Terrible rule for most everything else in life.)

953.
If I'm drunk and there's a rolling pin in sight,
WATCH OUT!
You're getting a spirited rendition of
"The Worst Pies in London."

954.
Did you hear about the Shakespearean Circus,
Aside Show?

955.
I can't do *The Sound of Music* because
I'm cloisterphobic.

956.
"I need to see *Our American Cousin* like I need
a hole in my head."
— Abraham Lincoln

957.

I was going to throw a small Tonys party,
but every Anthony I know is over 6 foot.

958.

I can never remember the name of
[Title of Show].

959.

If I were in *The Book of Mormon*,
I'd have to be Elder Lee.

960.

I love her so much,
I have to limit myself to just one Tyne Daly.

961.

I saw *Shout! The Mod Musical!*,
but I wish it had been *Shout! The Maude Musical.*

962.

My luck with theatre is so bad,
when I saw *The Phantom of the Opera*,
the chandelier fell down,
and they stopped the show for fifteen minutes.

963.

I just read *The Cherry Orchard*.
It's another play to Chekhov the list.

964.

I'm confident, if I had a laser pointer,
I could choreograph *CATS* in
fifteen minutes.

965.

"I will never cleave you!"
— Me, lying to my onions

966.

There's a musical version of
The Diary of Anne Frank.
Isn't hiding 8 people in an attic <u>without</u>
a 6-piece band hard enough?

967.

Shrek – The Musical is a modern-day example
of Commedia dell'farte.

968.

I don't own the album of *Anyone Can Whistle*
because I can't whistle,
and I won't listen to LIARS!

969.

I've always wanted to do *You're a Good Man,
Charlie Brown*, but I have a peanuts allergy.

970.

Be it comedy or hardware,
I'm a huge fan of Restoration.

971.

If Sutton ever goes crazy,
can we call her Bananas Foster?

972.

BD Wong just referenced *M. Butterfly*
on *Law & Order: SVU*.
Somewhere an angel just got their wings.

973.

Uncle Vanya = Realism
Miss Julie = Naturalism
Starmites = WTF-ism

974.

With a four-hour running time, they probably
should call it *Long Day's Journey into
Tomorrow Night*.

975.

I'm work-shopping a musical about a young girl's
pursuit of Chinese Theatre and her
parents' disapproval:
No Noh, Nanette!

976.

Growing up, my brothers listened to heavy metal.
I listened to *Steel Pier*, so that seems about right.

977.

"Show me on the doll where the musical
touched you."

— My Therapist

978.

Over the last few months, I've finished Ian's
bourbons and refilled the decanters with iced tea.
It works on stage.

979.

I'm doing a production of *Same Time, Next Year*,
but I'm doing it at a different time, next month,
so mark your calendars.

980.

I get that you can't pay last year's rent, and that
it will be hard to scrape together this year's rent,
but it should be your _goal_ to pay next year's rent.

981.

If you want my 2 cents,
use them as a down payment on
The 3 Penny Opera.

982.

ANDREW LLOYD WEBBER: Bet you can't name
more than 10 colors.
TIM RICE: Can too!
ANDREW LLOYD WEBBER: Nuh-uh!
TIM RICE: Yeah-huh!
(And musical theatre history is made.)

983.

If I were an Elizabethan drag queen,
I'd go by Titties Androgynous.

984.

Jello Dolly and *Aspics of Love* aren't great
musicals for vegans.

985.

Golden Rule of comedy:
Speak softly, and carry a big shtick.

986.

You're not an adult until you can completely
empathize with the Baroness Schraeder.

987.

My sex life is like *Hamilton*:
I just want to be in the room where it happens.

988.

I want to read through the theatrical canon,
but it sounds dangerous!

989.

Annie Get Your Gun would be a much different
musical if it were 'Warbucks' instead of 'Oakley'.

990.

I'd give my right arm to conduct a
Broadway musical.

991.

You'd think *Paddington: Live* would be an
extravaganza, but it starts with a bear stage.

992.

I'm all for Western medicine, and I'm all for
musical theatre, but it's time we re-evaluate the
science in Miss Adelaide's book.

993.

Hitler's favorite musical was
I Love You, You're Perfect, NOW CHANGE!

994.

Hitler's *least* favorite musical was,
Crazy for Jews.

995.

Many women audition for Christine in
The Phantom of the Opera, but few take home the
gold. It's just the way the Daaé is cast.

996.

To Bea Arthur, or not to Bea Arthur?
Is that even a question?

997.

I'm a fraud:
I saw *Once* twice.

998.

There's a huge difference between 'over-reacting'
and 'ovary acting'.
I have the *Vagina Monologues* ticket
stub to prove it.

999.

Fiddler on the Roof sounds like a workman's
comp claim waiting to happen.

1000.

You could never do *Dirty Dancing* in the round.
There'd be no corner in which nobody
could put Baby.

Epilogue
True Scenes from a Truly Gay Marriage

SCENE 1:
KASEY: My stomach hurts. I think I ate a bad pork chop.
IAN: Yay!
KASEY: Yay?
IAN: Skinny!
KASEY: True!

SCENE 2:
IAN: I took out the trash.
KASEY: You literally took out the trash? Or like, "Bitch, I took out the trash!" Like slang for "I yelled at them?"
IAN: I took out the trash.

SCENE 3:
KASEY: I think I got a computer virus.
IAN: Too much porn?
KASEY: I tried to download Patti LuPone's *Gypsy*.
IAN: You should just say porn.

SCENE 4:

KASEY: Make me another margarita, with just *this* much tequila.

IAN: (With his back turned) I assume your hands are three feet wide right now.

SCENE 5:

KASEY: We can't leave yet, I want to watch *The Barefoot Contessa!*

IAN: You've already seen this episode. It's the one where she makes chicken for Jeffery.

SCENE 6:

IAN: I mean, I know it's a movie, and I need to suspend my disbelief, but the whole thing seemed kind of implausible.

KASEY: It was *Finding Dory!!*

SCENE 7:

IAN: First of all –

KASEY: Oh, god. How many "of alls" are there going to be?

SCENE 8:

IAN: Your abs are fine. I've seen pictures of what they looked like.

SCENE 9:

KASEY: *(At Avenue Q)*: You're *my* purpose.
IAN: I'm so sorry.

SCENE 10:

KASEY: Is this joke too insensitive? "Between Glinda and Elphaba, *Wicked* is a *heroine* overdose."
IAN: Insensitive to whom? Heroin addicts or *Wicked* survivors?
KASEY: . . .

SCENE 11:

IAN: Watching you eat is like watching someone play *Hungry, Hungry Hippo.*

SCENE 12:

KASEY: Have you seen the Muppets preview? Fozzie's dating a girl!

IAN: You thought he'd be gay?

KASEY: Um...I thought he'd be dating a puppet.

SCENE 13:

IAN: (Driving and leaving a voicemail) Oh, look. There's a cow...So I was just thinking about you. Thought I'd call and say hi.

SCENE 14:

KASEY: My life devolves around you.

IAN: What?!?

KASEY: I mean *revolves!*

SCENE 15:

IAN: Ugh. Those high school girls at Starbucks™ are so annoying. "Is there sugar in this? I ordered it black." I must sound just like that when I order.

KASEY: To be fair, you *usually* sound just like a high school girl.

SCENE 16:

KASEY: Did you know Burger King is still cooking with trans fats?

IAN: (Paying not a whit of attention) I thought we were supposed to be supporting trans rights?

SCENE 17:

IAN: Have you seen...um, what's it called... *Kiss Me, I'm Asian?*

KASEY: (blink, blink) *The King and I?*

IAN: Yes!

SCENE 18:

(Discussing a play Kasey is writing)

IAN: Who dies?

KASEY: No one.

IAN: I like the new scene idea, but who dies again?

KASEY: No one dies! It's not f***ing *August: Osage County!*

IAN: Ok, I accept that. But can they at least *throw* something?

KASEY: Obviously.

SCENE 19:

KASEY: I'm getting so chunky.

IAN: You hurt your back. You'll get back to cardio and lose it eventually.

KASEY: (Withering glance)

IAN: I mean, you look great!

SCENE 20:

IAN: If I get Alzheimer's you have my permission to kill me in my sleep.

KASEY: Thank you. I was planning on it.

ACKNOWLEDGEMENTS

This book would not have been possible without the help and support of friends and family.

Thank you to my parents for instilling an unusually strong love of old-time radio and television; Yurel Echezarreta for keeping me grounded in *this* century too; Torrance Shepherd and Brad Frenette for laughing too hard and reading everything I sent their way; John West for always inspiring creativity. Ryan Worsing and Sam Rogers for never letting me get away with anything; Marco Pennette for his kindness and generosity; Jon Lutyens for teaching me the importance of brevity. (I know, I know, I'm wrapping it up...)

And Ian, who is everything I have ever wanted.

ABOUT THE AUTHOR

As the snow flew on a cold and grey Chicago mornin', another little baby child was born in... No, wait, that's an Elvis song.

Born in Spokane, Washington, Kasey RT Graham now calls New York City home. He lives there, with his husband, Ian, off and on. (To clarify: they live in the *city* off and on. As of publication, Kasey and Ian were definitely '*on*'.) Kasey is a theatre director and, as of four days ago, a writer.

They have no dogs or children, yet. Give it time, Mother!

Made in the USA
San Bernardino, CA
21 September 2016